THE MUSIC TREE
ACTIVITIES

PART 4

by
Frances Clark
Louise Goss
Sam Holland
Craig Sale

Educational Consultants:

Yat Yee Chong   Ted Cooper
Amy Glennon   Monica Hochstedler
Peter Jutras   Elvina Pearce
Mary Frances Reyburn   Craig Sale

ISBN-10: 1-58951-006-2
ISBN-13: 978-1-58951-006-7

PREFACE

We are proud to present this latest revision of **THE MUSIC TREE**, the most carefully researched and laboratory-tested series for elementary and intermediate piano students available.

This edition combines the best of the old and the new—a natural child-oriented sequence of learning experiences that has always been the hallmark of Frances Clark materials combined with new music of unprecedented variety and appeal. Great pedagogy and great music—a winning combination!

The elementary section of **THE MUSIC TREE** consists of the four parts listed below to be used in sequence. Each part has a textbook and an activities book to be used together:

TEXTBOOKS	ACTIVITIES BOOKS
TIME TO BEGIN (the primer)	**TIME TO BEGIN ACTIVITIES**
MUSIC TREE 1 (formerly A)	**ACTIVITIES 1**
MUSIC TREE 2A (formerly B)	**ACTIVITIES 2A**
MUSIC TREE 2B (formerly C)	**ACTIVITIES 2B**

Used together, these companion volumes provide a comprehensive plan for musical growth at the piano and prepare for the intermediate materials that follow in Parts 3 and 4.

The intermediate section of **THE MUSIC TREE** consists of **PART 3** (early intermediate) and **PART 4** (intermediate). Each part contains five correlated books to be used together.

THE MUSIC TREE PART 3 THE MUSIC TREE PART 4		ACTIVITIES PART 3 ACTIVITIES PART 4
KEYBOARD LITERATURE 3 **KEYBOARD LITERATURE 4** Exciting new collections of gems from the 17th, 18th, 19th and 20th centuries.	**STUDENTS' CHOICE 3** **STUDENTS' CHOICE 4** Winning collections of all-time recital favorites.	**KEYBOARD TECHNIC 3** **KEYBOARD TECHNIC 4** Comprehensive new compendia of essential exercises and etudes.

It is our hope that **THE MUSIC TREE** will provide for you the same success and delight in teaching that we have experienced and that your students will share with ours the excitement of this new adventure in learning.

As you start MUSIC TREE PART 4, you are also ready for the Part 4 companion volumes: ACTIVITIES PART 4, KEYBOARD LITERATURE PART 4, KEYBOARD TECHNIC PART 4 and STUDENTS' CHOICE PART 4.

We have provided correlations between MUSIC TREE and ACTIVITIES at the bottom of the first page in each unit. In addition, you will find page-by-page correlations among MUSIC TREE, KEYBOARD LITERATURE, STUDENTS' CHOICE and KEYBOARD TECHNIC. These are found in the outside borders of each page.

CONTENTS

Theory

Relative Major and Minor Keys—A Review

Every key signature can show two related keys: a MAJOR key and a RELATIVE MINOR key.

Relative major and minor keys use
the **same notes** but have **different tonics**.
*The relative minor is found 3 half steps
below the major tonic.*

Identify each of these key signatures:
- as the major key
- as the relative minor key

_____MAJOR _____MINOR   _____MAJOR _____MINOR   _____MAJOR _____MINOR

Relative Keys - D Major and B Minor

D major and B minor are relative keys. The key of B minor is built on the **6th degree** of D major.

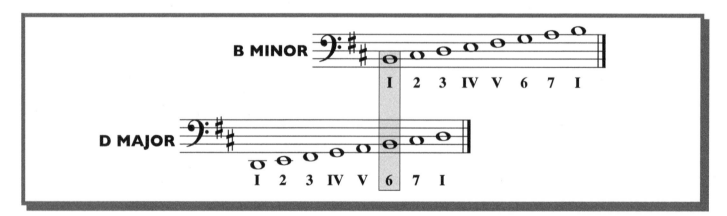

When the minor scale uses the same notes as the relative major key, it is called a
NATURAL MINOR scale. In minor keys, the 7th degree is often raised **one half step**.
When the 7th degree is raised, it is called a HARMONIC MINOR scale.

I 2 3 IV V 6 7 I   V

Relative Keys - B-flat Major and G Minor

B-flat major and G minor are relative keys.

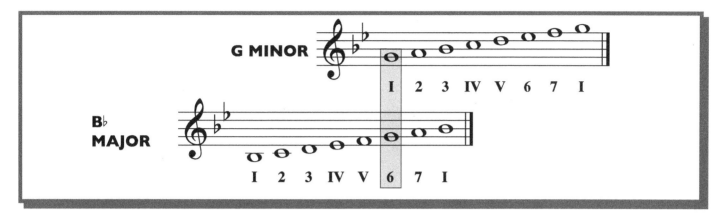

Draw the G minor scale in the harmonic form:
- raise the 7th degree by drawing a sharp
- write the dominant triad above **V**
- add a sharp to make the triad major

Accompanying and Transposing Using **I**, **IV** and **V7**

In **MUSIC TREE 3**, you learned to accompany melodies using **I**, **IV** and **V7**.

As a review, accompany *The Muffin Man*:
- for parts made mostly of **I** triad tones use **I**
- for parts made mostly of **IV** triad tones use **IV**
- for parts made mostly of **V** triad tones use **V7**

The Muffin Man is in the key of _____major.

I is _____.   **IV** is _____.   **V** is _____.

The Muffin Man

English

Now transpose *The Muffin Man* with your accompaniment to the keys of C major and F major.

Learning about

In **MUSIC TREE 3** you learned

the rhythm pattern:

Here is the opposite pattern:

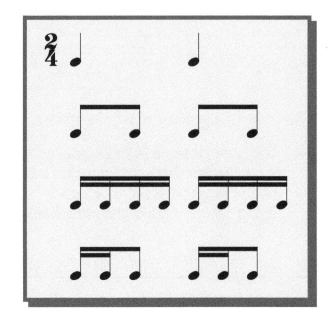

1. Swing and say the rhyme with a strong rhythmic pulse,
   one full arm swing for each pulse.

Polly, Put the Kettle On

Pol-ly, put the ket-tle on,   Pol-ly put the ket-tle on,   Pol-ly put the ket-tle on, we'll all have tea.

Su-key, take it off a-gain,   Su-key take it off a-gain,   Su-key take it off a-gain, they've all gone a-way.

2. Say the rhyme again, making dashes under the words
   one dash for each pulse.

3. Then walk the rhythm as you say the rhyme,
   taking one step for each pulse.

6

Counting

In each of these rhythms, set a strong rhythmic pulse:

1. Point and count.

2. Tap and count.

Playing

Before playing each of these pieces:

1. Point and count.

2. Tap and count.

Sight-Playing

Before playing each piece, observe the key and time signatures.
Then set a strong rhythmic pulse.

Desert Sands is in the key of _____ major / minor (circle one).

Desert Sands

Sailor's Dance is in the key of _____ major / minor (circle one).

Sailor's Dance

Determination is in the key of _____ major / minor (circle one).

Determination

Hidden Tunes

There are two well-known tunes hidden on this page.

To discover them, write the interval, shown by the number, **below** each note.

Then play the tune you wrote and write the title on the line above the tune.

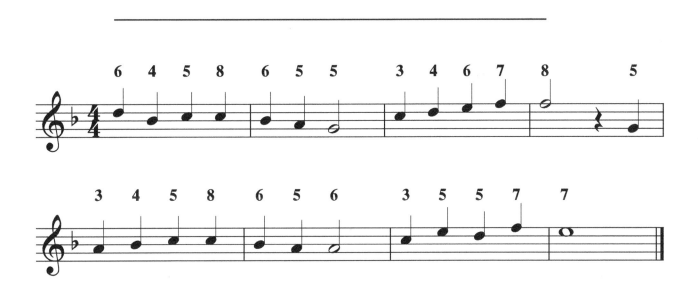

Theory

Relative Keys—A Major and F# Minor

The key of A major begins a 5th **above** D.

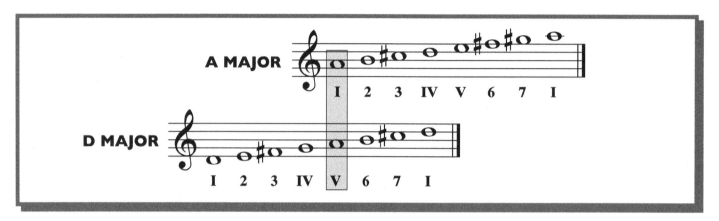

On this keyboard, write the A major scale.
- write the name on each key
- number the degrees
- mark the two half steps

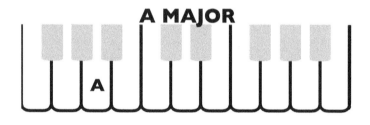

Trace this A major key signature.

Now write the A major key signature.

A major and F# minor are relative keys.

The key of F# minor is built on the **6th degree** of A Major.

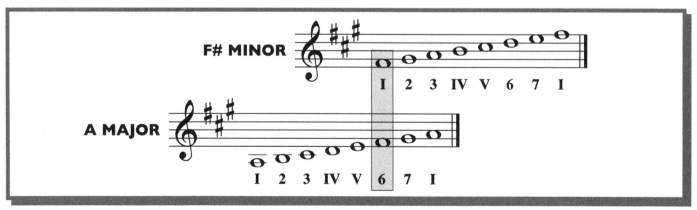

For correlated Discoveries, Repertoire and Technic see MUSIC TREE 4, pages 11-16.

On this keyboard, write the F# minor scale.
- use HARMONIC FORM
- write the name on each key
- number the degrees
- mark the three half steps

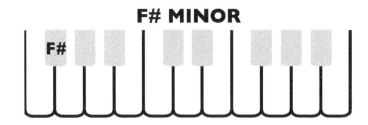

F# MINOR

F#

Because they are relative keys, the F# minor key signature is the same as A major.

Inversions of Triads—A Review

For each triad:
1. Draw the inversions on the staff.
2. Darken the root tone in each inversion.

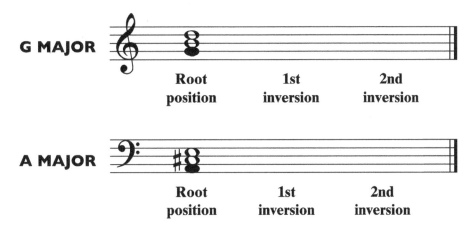

G MAJOR

| Root position | 1st inversion | 2nd inversion |

A MAJOR

| Root position | 1st inversion | 2nd inversion |

Accompanying and Transposing Using I, IV and V7

Here is a melody to accompany with **I**, **IV** and **V7**.
Follow the directions on page 5.

Bingo is in the key of _____ major.

I is _____.   **IV** is _____.   **V** is _____.

Bingo

Traditional

Now transpose *Bingo* with your accompaniment to the keys of G major and C major.

Rhythm

Counting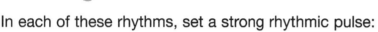

In each of these rhythms, set a strong rhythmic pulse:

1. Point and count the harder part.

2. Tap and count hands together.

1.

2.

Rhythm Detective

Add measure bars and an ending bar to each of these rhythms.

1.

2.

Find and circle the measures that have too many pulses.

1.

2.

Ear Detective

Your teacher will play a **3rd** or a **6th**.
Circle the interval you hear.

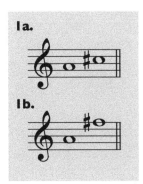

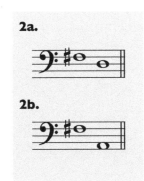

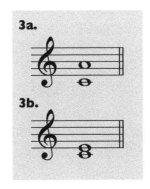

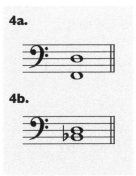

Your teacher will play either a **natural** or a **harmonic** minor scale.
Circle the one you hear.

| **1a.** natural | **2a.** natural | **3a.** natural |
| **1b.** harmonic | **2b.** harmonic | **3b.** harmonic |

Your teacher will play either a **major** or a **minor** chord progression.
Circle the one you hear.

| **1a.** major | **2a.** major | **3a.** major | **4a.** major |
| **1b.** minor | **2b.** minor | **3b.** minor | **4b.** minor |

Your teacher will tap one rhythm from each of these pairs.
Circle the pattern you hear.

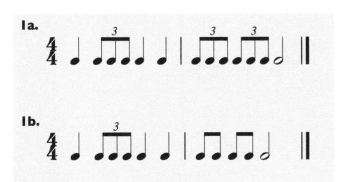

Sight-Playing

Before playing each piece, observe the key and time signatures.
Then set a strong rhythmic pulse.

Irish Tune is in the key of _____ major / minor (circle one).
    The LH plays _____ and _____ chords.

Irish Tune

A Mystery is in the key of _____ major / minor (circle one).
    Which form of the scale does it use? natural / harmonic (circle one).

A Mystery

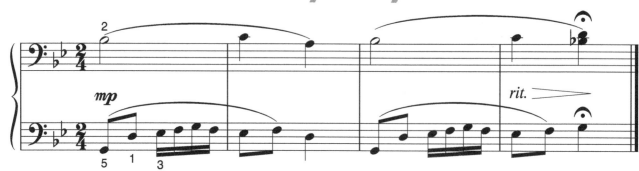

Holiday Bells is in the key of _____ major / minor (circle one).
    The LH plays _____ and _____ chords.

Holiday Bells

Maze

Find your way through the maze by following the notes of the **A major scale** in ascending order.

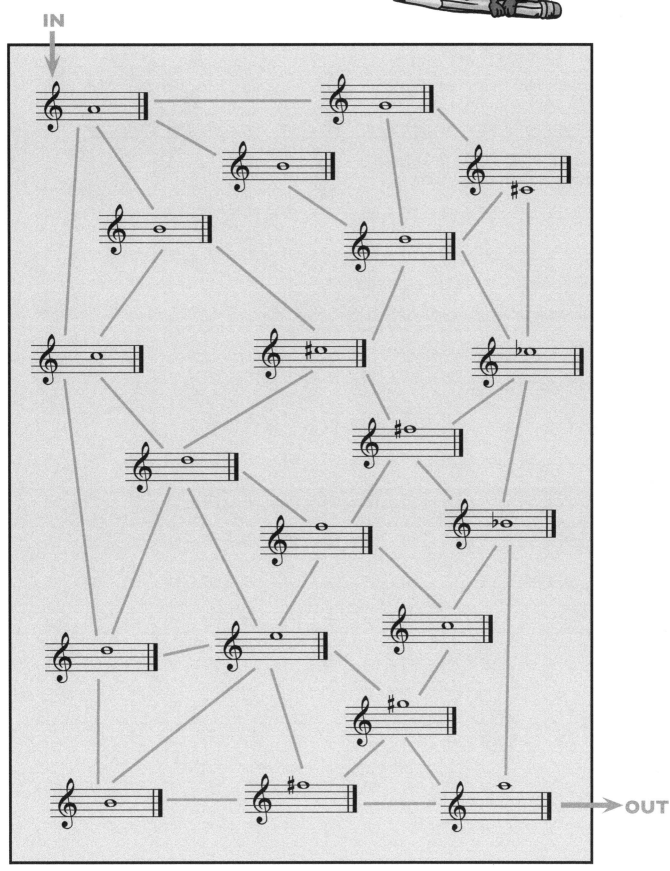

Theory

Accompanying Using Letter Symbols

Letter symbols are another way to show which chord to play when accompanying a melody. This method is common in folk and popular music.

When letter symbols are used:

- a capital letter shows a **major** triad in root position.

- a capital letter with an "m" shows a **minor** triad in root position.

The Ash Grove is in the key of _____ major.

When you can play the melody easily:

1. Practice the LH chord changes until they are secure.

2. Play hands together.

The Ash Grove

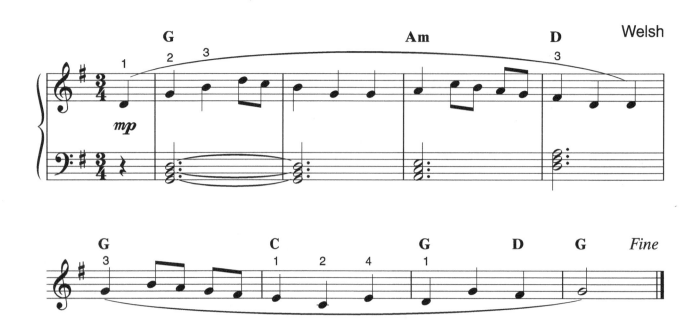

For correlated Discoveries, Repertoire and Technic see MUSIC TREE 4, pages 17-23.

Identifying Chords

Play each chord, then label it with its letter symbol.

1.

2.

3.

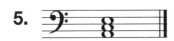
4.

5.

6.

Minor Keys and Scales

On this staff:
- identify the minor key
- write the **natural** minor scale

_____ **MINOR**

On this staff:
- identify the minor key
- write the **harmonic** minor scale

_____ **MINOR**

Rhythm

More about Syncopation

In **MUSIC TREE 3**, you learned that syncopation is a shift in rhythmic emphasis from a strong part of the pulse to a part that is normally weaker.

A type of syncopation, often found in rock music, uses a tie over the barline:

In each of these rhythms, set a strong rhythmic pulse:

    1. Point and count.
    2. Tap and count.

1.

2.

Crazy Rhythms

In each of the rhythms below:

    1. Tap and count the RH part.
    2. Tap and count hands together.
    3. Tap, snap and count.
        ♩ = TAP   ■ = SNAP

1.

2.

Ear Detective

Your teacher will tap one rhythm from each of these pairs.
Circle the pattern you hear.

1a.

2a.

1b.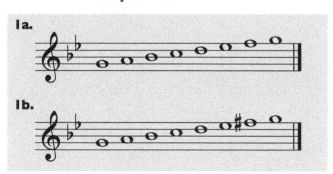

2b.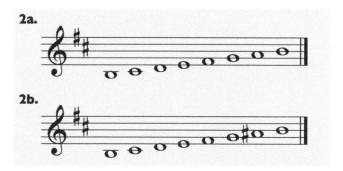

Your teacher will play either a **2nd** or a **7th**.
Circle the interval you hear.

1a.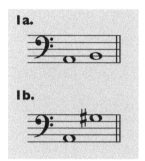

2a.

3a.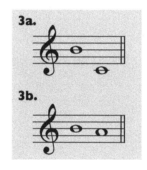

4a.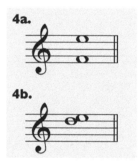

1b.

2b.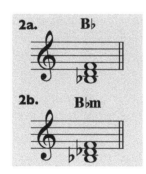

3b.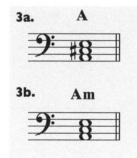

4b.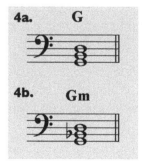

Your teacher will play either a **major** or a **minor** triad.
Circle the triad you hear.

1a. D

2a. B♭

3a. A

4a. G

1b. Dm

2b. B♭m

3b. Am

4b. Gm

Your teacher will play either a or minor scale.
Circle the scale you hear.

1a.

2a.

1b.

2b.

Sight-Playing

Before playing each piece, observe the key and time signatures.
Then set a strong rhythmic pulse.

Horn Call uses the _____ major triad and inversions.

Horn Call

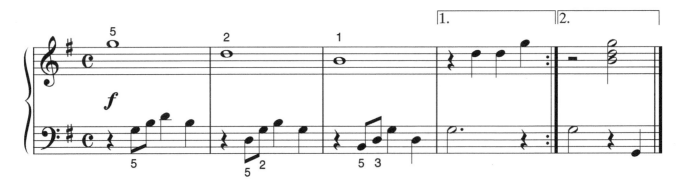

Springtime is in the key of _____ major / minor (circle one).

Springtime

Home Run is in the key of _____ major / minor (circle one).

Home Run

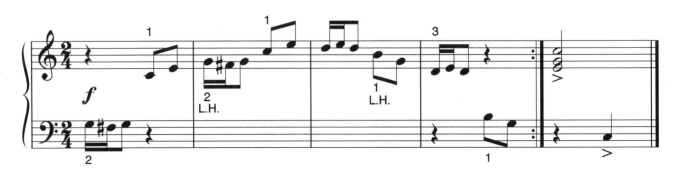

 $\frac{4}{4}$ is often shown as **c**, usually called "common time."

Crossword Puzzle

ACROSS

2. Notes of a G natural minor scale (include #'s and ♭'s)

5. **IV** triad tones in F major

7. (music notation)

9. Relative major key of A minor

10. Relative minor key of F major

11. (music notation)

DOWN

1. Minor scale form with raised 7th degree

3. 6/8 for example

4. **V** triad tones in C major

6. (music notation)

8. Letter symbol for (music notation)

12. Letter symbol for (music notation)

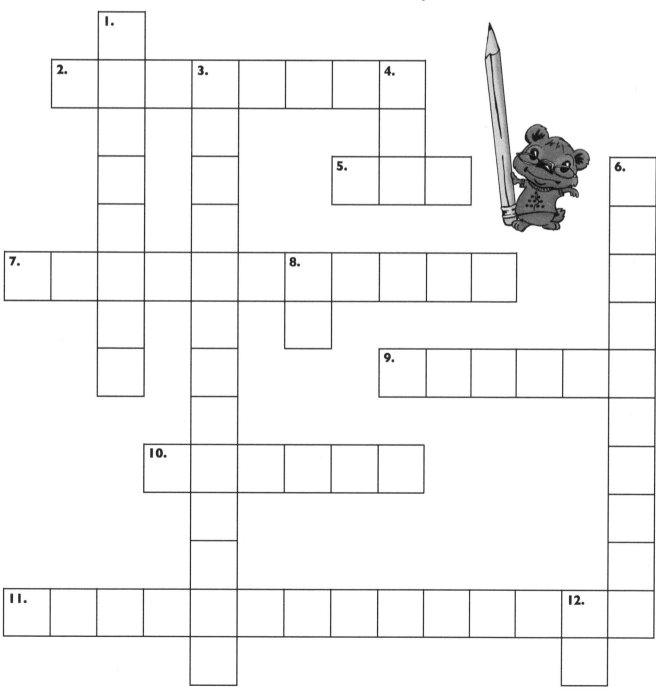

Theory

Relative Keys—E-flat Major and C Minor

The key of E-flat major begins a 5th **below** B-flat.

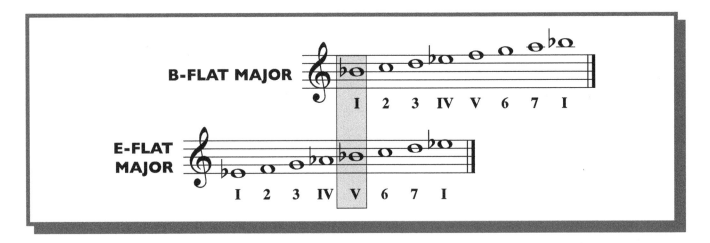

On this keyboard, write the E-flat major scale.
- write the name on each key
- number the degrees
- mark the two half steps

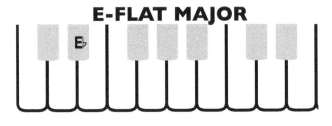

Trace this E-flat major key signature.

Now write the E-flat major key signature.

E-flat major and C minor are relative keys.
The key of C minor is built on the **6th degree** of E-flat major.

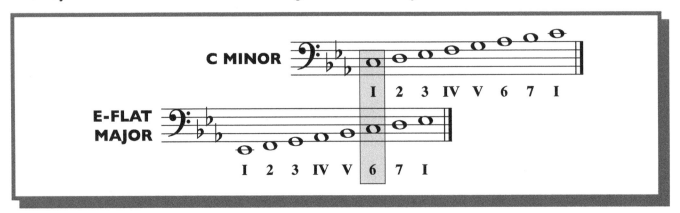

On this keyboard, write the C minor scale in harmonic form.
- Write the name on each key.
  (Use a natural to raise the 7th degree.)
- Number the degrees.
- Mark the three half steps.

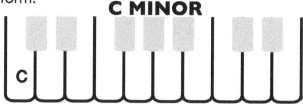

Accompanying Using Letter Symbols

Pastorale is in the key of _____ major.

When you can play the melody easily:
1. Practice the LH chord changes until they are secure.
2. Play hands together.

Pastorale

Beethoven

Ear Detective

Your teacher will play a 2nd, 3rd, 6th or 7th.
Circle the interval you hear.

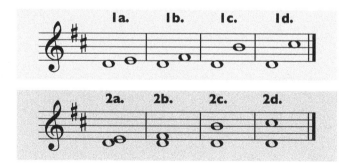

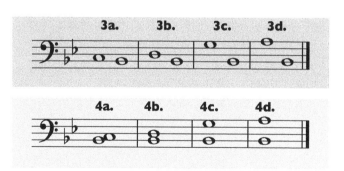

Your teacher will play either a **major** or a **minor** triad.
Circle the one you hear.

1a. C   **2a.** F   **3a.** E   **4a.** B

1b. Cm   **2b.** Fm   **3b.** Em   **4b.** Bm

Rhythm

Learning about Meters with a Half-Note Pulse

Set a strong ♩ pulse, then clap and count this rhythm:

How many ♩ pulses are in each measure? _____

How many ♩ values are in each measure? _____

Clap and count the rhythm again, this time feeling a ♩ as the pulse:

In meters with a half-note pulse, the bottom number of the time signature is a **2**.
For example:

2/2 = two ♩ pulses per measure   **3/2** = three ♩ pulses per measure

The time signature **2/2** can also be written ¢. This is usually called ⬚cut time.⬚

Counting Meters with a Half-Note Pulse

In each of these rhythms, set a strong **half-note** pulse:

1. Point and count.

2. Tap and count.

Rhythm Detective

Write the time signature (♩ pulse) for each rhythm in the box provided.

1.

2.

Add measure bars and an ending bar to each of these rhythms.

1.

2.

Pulse Play

Play and count each piece two times:
first counting a **quarter-note** pulse
then counting a **half-note** pulse

1.

2.

3.

Sight-Playing

Before playing each piece, observe the key and time signatures.
Then set a strong rhythmic pulse.

Ancient Times is in the key of _____ major / minor (circle one).
    Which form of the scale does it use? natural / harmonic (circle one).

Ancient Times

In the Henhouse is in the key of _____ major / minor (circle one).

In the Henhouse

Fanfare uses the _____ major triad and inversions.

Fanfare

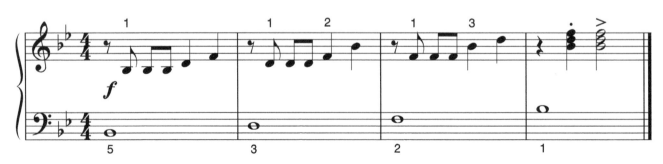

26

Matching Keys

Draw lines to match each key signature with
the **major** and **relative minor** key it represents.

C MAJOR		B MINOR
Eb MAJOR		D MINOR
G MAJOR		A MINOR
A MAJOR		F# MINOR
D MAJOR		C MINOR
Bb MAJOR		E MINOR
F MAJOR		G MINOR

Theory

The Pentatonic Scale

The PENTATONIC SCALE uses only five notes.
It is found in folk music from Asia to the British Isles.

The easiest pentatonic scale to see
is the one that begins on G-flat
and uses the five black keys.

A pentatonic scale can also use white keys.
It is just like a major scale
but without degrees 4 and 7.

On each staff:
- cross out degrees 4 and 7
- play the remaining pentatonic scale

G PENTATONIC

F PENTATONIC

A PENTATONIC

More about Letter Symbols

When using letter symbols, inversions are indicated
by writing the bottom note of the inversion
after the chord name.

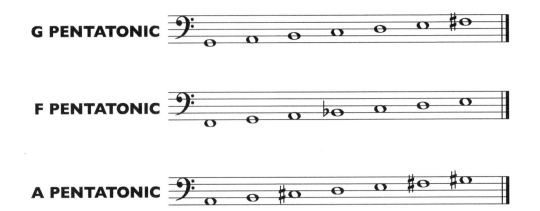

C/E   C/G

On each keyboard, mark an X on each key of the chord indicated by the letter symbol.

G/B   **D/F#**   **Cm/G**

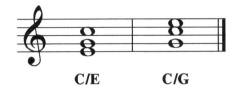

For correlated Discoveries, Repertoire and Technic see MUSIC TREE 4, pages 31-37.

Accompanying Using Letter Symbols

London's Bells is in the key of _____ major.

When you can play the melody easily:
1. Practice the LH chord changes until they are secure.
2. Play hands together.

Ear Detective

Your teacher will play either a **4th** or a **5th**.
Circle the interval you hear.

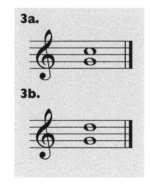
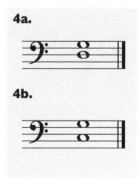

Your teacher will play a chord progression using **I**, **IV** and **V7**.
Circle the progression you hear.

1a. I IV I V7 I

1b. I IV IV V7 I

2a. I V7 I V7 I

2b. I V7 IV V7 I

3a. I IV IV V7 I

3b. I IV V7 V7 I

Rhythm

Learning about

A dotted eighth note  fills the time of an eighth note tied to a sixteenth note.

A dotted eighth note followed by a sixteenth note

lasts as long as one quarter note

1. Point and count.

2. Tap and count.

1. Swing and say the words with a strong rhythmic pulse, one full arm swing for each pulse.

Battle Hymn of the Republic

Glo - ry, glo - ry hal - le - lu - jah! Glo - ry, glo - ry hal - le - lu - jah!

Glo - ry, glo - ry hal - le - lu - jah! His truth is march - ing on.

2. Say the words again, making dashes under the words□one dash for each pulse.

3. Then walk the rhythm as you say the rhyme, taking one step for each pulse.

Counting

In each of these rhythms, set a strong rhythmic pulse:

1. Point and count

2. Tap and count.

Playing

Before playing each of these pieces:

1. Point and count.

2. Tap and count.

Sight-Playing

Before playing each piece, observe the key and time signatures.
Then set a strong rhythmic pulse.

Mountain Ballad is in the key of _____ major / minor (circle one).

Mountain Ballad

Vacation is in the key of _____ major / minor (circle one).

Vacation

A Special Event is in the key of _____ major / minor (circle one).

A Special Event

Word Search

Circle the word that corresponds to each symbol or clue.
The word may go forward, backward, up, down or diagonally.

1. Scale with 5 notes

2. **Bm**, **G/D** for example

3. Relative key of F major

4. **V**

5. **I** triad tones in A minor

6. Relative key of E♭ major

7. ¢

8. Minor scale form with raised 7th degree

9. **I**

10. The pulse in $\frac{3}{2}$, $\frac{2}{2}$, etc.

11.

C	U	T	T	I	M	E	P	Q	R
I	I	B	A	D	C	T	F	E	S
N	G	N	I	H	K	O	J	M	L
O	N	P	O	R	Q	N	T	S	O
T	V	U	X	M	W	F	Z	Y	B
A	C	E	C	A	R	L	D	B	M
T	E	C	F	O	D	A	G	E	Y
N	A	F	N	H	I	H	H	A	S
E	Z	I	W	Y	X	R	V	M	R
P	M	W	U	P	O	S	M	A	E
D	O	M	I	N	A	N	T	J	T
K	G	J	I	L	C	I	N	O	T
R	P	M	A	D	G	C	F	R	E
X	C	Y	R	S	V	Y	E	N	L

Theory

The Blues Scale

One of the most popular scales in jazz is called the BLUES SCALE.

Here is the blues scale in C.

On this keyboard:
- Mark an X on each key of the C blues scale

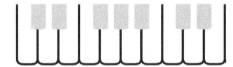

A minor 3rd and a whole step appear at the bottom and top of the blues scale and are connected by two half steps.

On each keyboard, write the blues scale:
- Mark an X on each key
- circle the minor 3rds

D BLUES SCALE   **G BLUES SCALE**

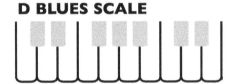

In blues, it is common for melodies to add notes that change the minor 3rds to major.

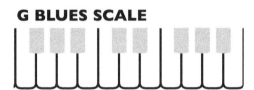

On each blues scale:
- circle the minor 3rds
- write the notes that change the **minor** 3rds to **major**

D BLUES SCALE   **G BLUES SCALE**

Accompanying Using **I, IV** and **V7**

Auld Lang Syne uses the F pentatonic scale.
Accompany this melody with **I, IV** and **V7** chords.
Follow the directions on page 5.

I is _____.   **IV** is _____.   **V7** is _____.

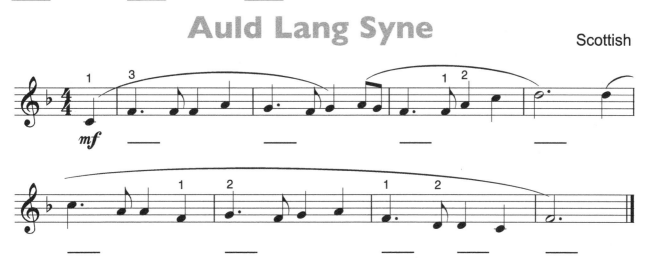

Auld Lang Syne

Scottish

Now transpose *Auld Lang Syne* with your accompaniment to the key of G major.

Ear Detective

Your teacher will play a 2nd, 3rd, 4th, 5th, 6th or 7th. Circle the interval you hear.

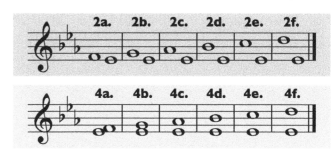

Your teacher will play either a **pentatonic** or a **blues** scale. Circle the one you hear.

1a. pentatonic   **2a.** pentatonic   **3a.** pentatonic
1b. blues   **2b.** blues   **3b.** blues

Your teacher will tap one rhythm from each of these pairs. Circle the pattern you hear.

Rhythm

Counting

In each of these rhythms, set a strong rhythmic pulse:
1. Point and count the harder part.
2. Tap and count hands together.

Rhythm Detective

Add measure bars and an ending bar to each of these rhythms.

Crazy Rhythms

In each of the rhythms below:
1. Point and count.
2. Tap, clap and count

= CLAP your hands   = TAP the KEYBOARD COVER

= TAP your HEAD   = TAP your LAP

Set a slow tempo. When secure, try it faster!

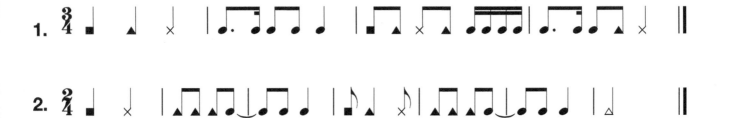

Sight-Playing

Before playing each piece, observe the key and time signatures.
Then set a strong rhythmic pulse.

Song is in the key of _____ major / minor (circle one).

Each measure has _____ half-note pulses.

Song

The Hunt uses the _____ major triad and inversions.

The Hunt

Cherry Blossoms uses a _____ scale.

Cherry Blossoms

Puzzling Triads

Spell each triad or inversion indicated by the letter symbol.
Write the letters in the boxes provided.
Then use the circled letters to complete the answer at the bottom of the page.

1.

   E♭/B♭

2.

   Gm/B♭

3.

   Em

4.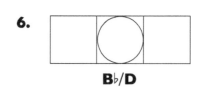

   A

5.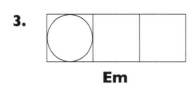

   Am/E

6.

   B♭/D

7.

   C

How do you quickly find a major key's relative minor key?

___ O ___ O W N T H R ___ ___ H ___ L ___ S T ___ P S

  1   2   3 4   5 6   7

Theory

Mixolydian Mode

In ancient music, there was a system of scales with Greek names called MODES.
Like major and minor scales, modes use a special arrangement of whole steps and half steps.

The MIXOLYDIAN MODE is made of the white keys from G to G.

It is the same as a major scale, except the 7th degree is a half step lower.

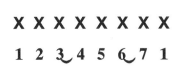

X X X X X X X

1 2 3 4 5 6 7 1

1 2 3 4 5 6 7 1

In Mixolydian mode, the half steps are between degrees ___ - ___ and ___ - ___.

Change each major scale to Mixolydian mode.
- Lower the 7th degree by adding a flat or a natural.
- Play the Mixolydian mode.

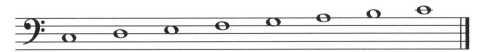

On each keyboard, build a Mixolydian mode.
- Write the name on each key.

MIXOLYDIAN MODE
(on A)

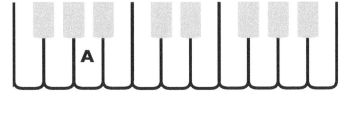

MIXOLYDIAN MODE
(on B-FLAT)

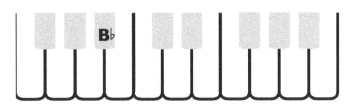

For correlated Discoveries, Repertoire and Technic see MUSIC TREE 4, pages 43-48.

Accompanying Using Letter Symbols

Sailor's Dance uses the Mixolydian mode built on A.

When you can play the melody easily:

1. Practice the LH chords.

2. Play both hands together.

Sailor's Dance

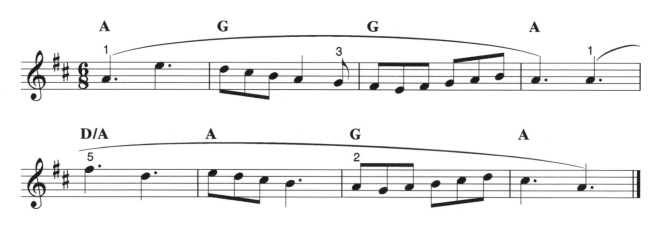

Rhythm

Rhythm Jumble

Circle the rhythms that have three quarter note pulses.
1. Write them in any order in the blank measures below.
2. Clap and count the rhythm you created.

Rhythm Detective

Complete each incomplete measure with one note.

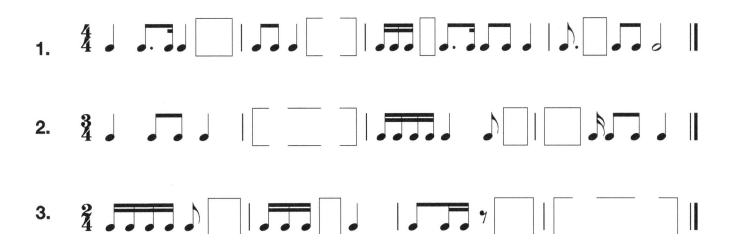

Pulse Play

Draw a line to connect the boxes on the left (𝅗𝅥 pulse) to the boxes
on the right (♩ pulse) that have the same rhythm.

Clap and count each pair to check your work.

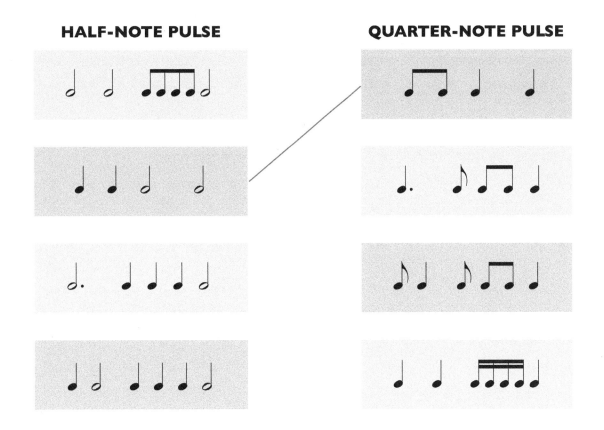

Ear Detective

Your teacher will play a 2nd, 3rd, 4th, 5th, 6th or 7th **above** the notes given.
Label the interval in the space below.
Write the second note on the staff.

Your teacher will play a 2nd, 3rd, 4th, 5th, 6th or 7th **below** the notes given.
Label the interval in the space below.
Write the second note on the staff.

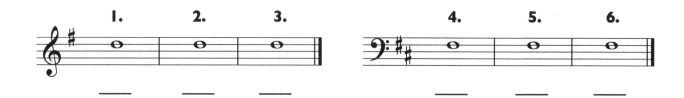

Your teacher will play either a **Mixolydian** mode or a **major** scale.
Circle the pattern you hear.

| **1a.** Mixolydian | **2a.** Mixolydian | **3a.** Mixolydian |
| **1b.** major | **2b.** major | **3b.** major |

Your teacher will tap the rhythms below. Some measures are incomplete.
Write the missing rhythm you hear.

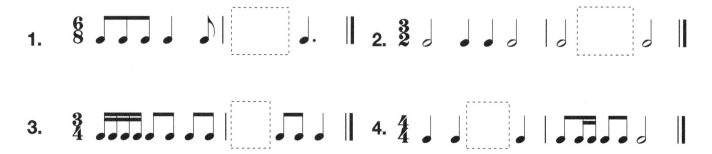

Sight-Playing

Before playing each piece, observe the key and time signatures.
Then set a strong rhythmic pulse.

Musette is in the key of _____ major / minor (circle one).

Musette

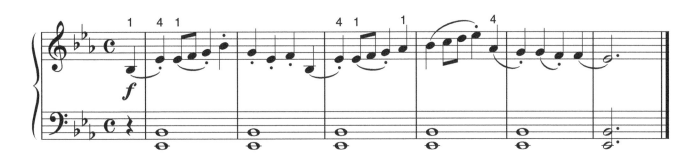

Alla Tarantella is in the key of _____ major / minor (circle one).

In measures 3-6, the LH plays _____, _____ and _____ chords.

Alla Tarantella

Rock Ballad is in the key of _____ major / minor (circle one).

Rock Ballad

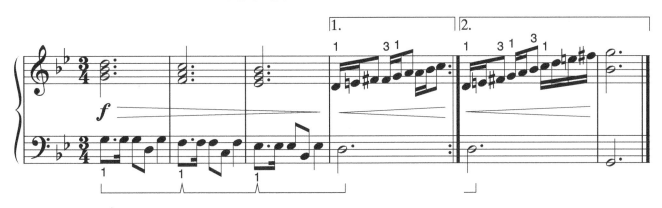

43

Scale Repair

Each of these scales is incorrect.
Add sharps or flats to correct each scale.

A MAJOR

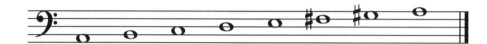

D MINOR
(natural form)

G MINOR
(harmonic form)

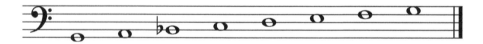

PENTATONIC SCALE
(on D)

MIXOLYDIAN MODE
(on F)

Theory

Scales and Modes

On each keyboard, build the scale by writing the name on each key.

BLUES SCALE
(on F)

PENTATONIC SCALE
(on A)

MIXOLYDIAN MODE
(on B-FLAT)

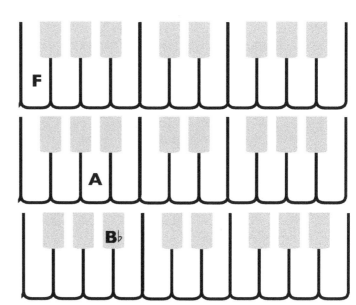

Accompanying Using I, IV and V7 in Minor

Here is a melody in a minor key to accompany with **I**, **IV** and **V7** chords.
In minor keys the **I** and **IV** chords are minor.

Dame Get Up is in the key of _____ minor.
I is _____.   **IV** is _____.   **V** is _____.

Dame Get Up

English

Now transpose *Dame Get Up* with your accompaniment to the key of C minor.

For correlated Discoveries, Repertoire and Technic see MUSIC TREE 4, pages 49-54.

Rhythm

Learning about ♫ in Compound Meter

Three pairs of sixteenth notes

fill the time of **three** eighth notes

or of **one** dotted quarter note.

The rhythmic pattern

is usually written:

1. Emphasize the ♩. pulse (counts 1 and 4) with your voice as you clap and count.

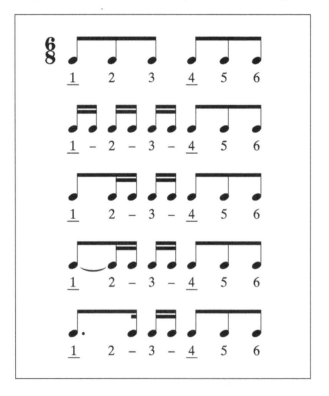

2. Count the rhythm again, making dashes under the notes—one dash for each pulse.

3. Walk and count the rhythm, taking one step for each pulse.

Counting ♫♪ in Compound Meter

In each of these rhythms, set a strong rhythmic pulse:

1. Point and count the RH.

2. Tap and count hands together.

Playing ♪♫ in Compound Meter

Before playing each of these pieces:

1. Point and count.

2. Tap and count.

Twirling

Bear Dance

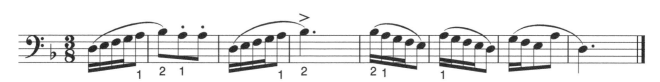

Ear Detective

Your teacher will play the melodies below. Some measures are incomplete.
Write the missing notes you hear.

Your teacher will play either a **Mixolydian** mode or a **major** scale.
Circle the one you hear.

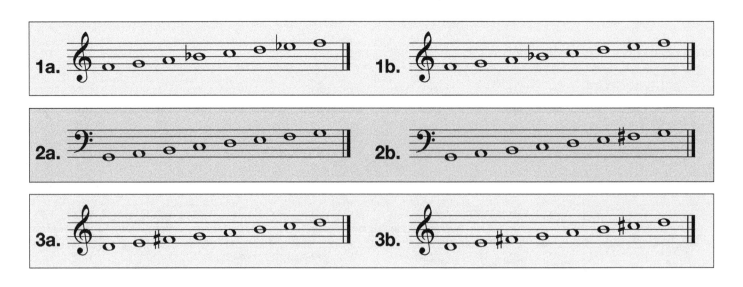

Your teacher will tap the following rhythms. Some measures are blank.
Write the rhythm you hear in the blank measures.

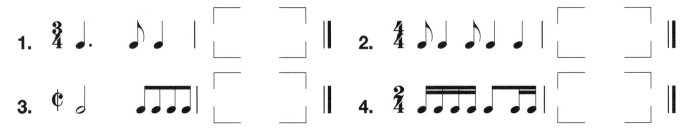

48

Sight-Playing

Before playing each piece, observe the key and time signatures.
Then set a strong rhythmic pulse.

Ceremonial March uses the G _____ mode.

Ceremonial March

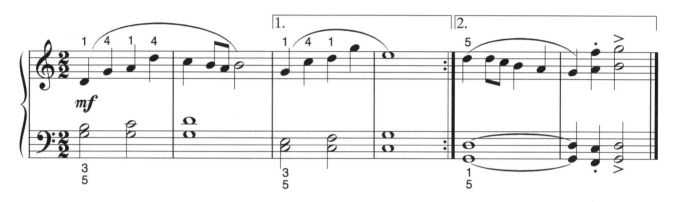

Blues in C uses notes from the C and F blues scales.

Blues in C

Canon is in the key of _____ major / minor (circle one).

Canon

Crossword Puzzle

ACROSS

2. F/C

4. Relative key of E-flat major

6.

10. Scale with 5 notes

11. Letter symbol for

12. Relative key of F# minor

DOWN

1.

3. Notes of Mixolydian mode on A (include sharps)

5. Em/B

7. Dm/A

8. ¢

9. Am

Theory

Dorian Mode

The DORIAN MODE is made of the white keys from D to D.
It is the same as a natural minor scale, except the 6th degree is a half step higher.

X X X X X X X
1 2 3 4 5 6 7 1

1 2 3 4 5 6 7 1

In Dorian mode, the half steps are between degrees ____-____ and ____-____.

Change each natural minor scale to Dorian mode:
* Raise the 6th degree by adding a sharp or natural.
* Play the Dorian mode.

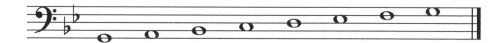

On each keyboard, build a Dorian mode.
* Write the name on each key

DORIAN MODE (on C)

DORIAN MODE (on A)

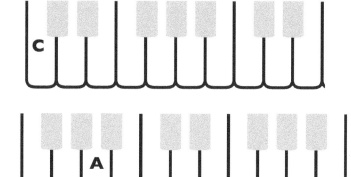

For correlated Discoveries, Repertoire and Technic see MUSIC TREE 4, pages 55-59.

Letter Symbols for **V7**

When using letter symbols, **V7** chord inversions are also shown by writing the bottom note of the inversion after the chord name.

On each keyboard, mark an X on each key of the chord indicated by the letter symbol.

D7/F#

D7/A

D7/C

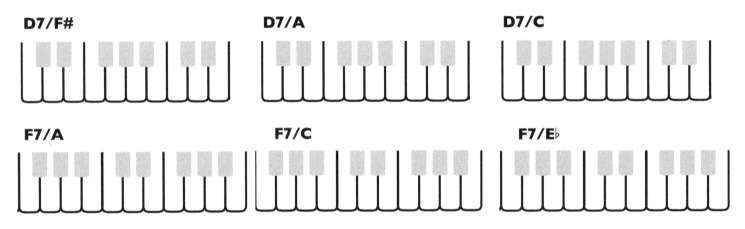

F7/A

F7/C

F7/E♭

Accompanying Using Letter Symbols

Now Is the Month of Maying is in the key of _____ major.
It uses letter symbols for **V7** chords.

When you can play the melody easily:
1. Practice the LH chord changes until they are secure.
2. Play hands together.

Now Is the Month of Maying

52

Rhythm

Crazy Rhythms

In each of the rhythms:

    1. Tap and count each hand alone.

    2. Tap and count hands together.

♩ = Tap on KEYBOARD COVER

✗ = Tap your HEAD

Set a slow steady tempo. When secure, try it faster!

1.

2.

Pulse Play

Each box contains a rhythm with three beats.
The meter for each column uses a different basic pulse.
- Draw lines to connect the boxes that have the same rhythm.
- Clap and count each set of boxes to check your work.

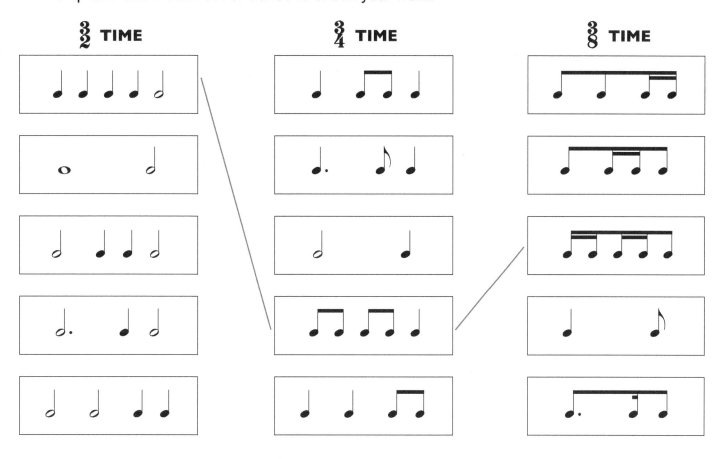

Ear Detective

Your teacher will play the melodies below. Some measures are incomplete.
Write the missing notes you hear.

Your teacher will play either a **Dorian** mode or a **natural minor** scale.
Circle the pattern you hear.

1a. Dorian	**2a.** Dorian	**3a.** Dorian
1b. natural minor	**2b.** natural minor	**3b.** natural minor

Your teacher will tap the following rhythms. Some measures are incomplete.
Write the missing rhythm you hear.

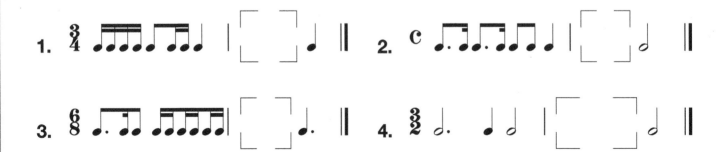

54

Sight-Playing

Before playing each piece, observe the key and time signatures.
Then set a strong rhythmic pulse.

Courtly Dance uses the G _____ mode.

Courtly Dance

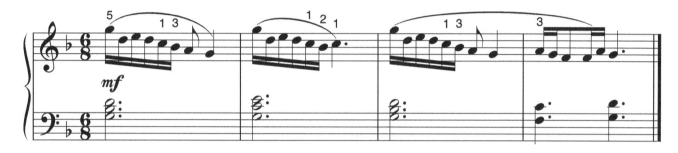

Anticipation is in the key of _____ major / minor (circle one).

Anticipation

Jubilation uses the F _____ mode.

Jubilation

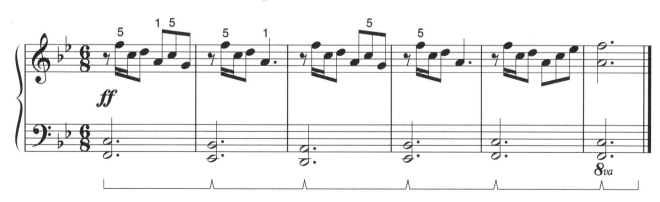

Rhythm Maze

Find your way through the maze by following the patterns that are in **6/8** time.

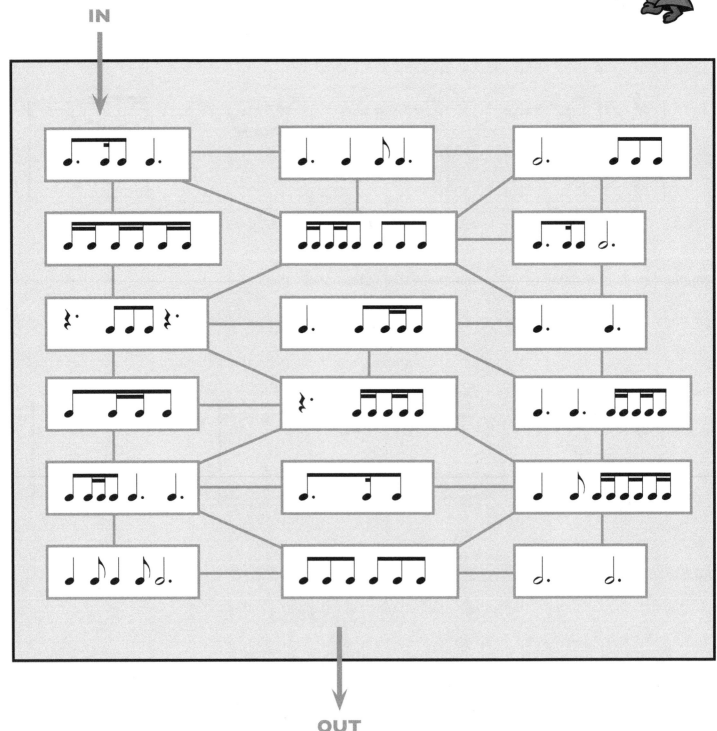

Now tap and count your way through the maze non-stop.

Theory

Accompanying Using Letter Symbols

Scarborough Fair uses the _____mode built on D.
When you can play the melody easily:
1. Practice the LH chords.
2. Play hands together.

Scarborough Fair

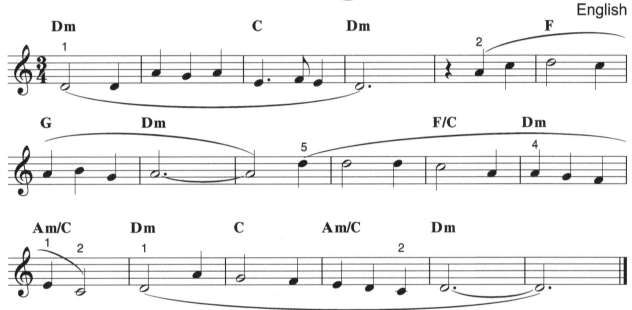

Accompanying Using I, IV and V7

Here is a melody to accompany with **I, IV** and **V7** chords.
Sicilian Dance is in the key of _____ major / minor (circle one).

I is _____.   **IV** is _____.   **V** is _____.

Sicilian Dance

Now transpose *Sicilian Dance* with your accompaniment to the key of D minor.

For correlated Discoveries, Repertoire and Technic see MUSIC TREE 4, pages 60-64.

Rhythm

Rhythm Jumble

Circle the rhythms that have four quarter-note pulses.
  1. Write them in any order in the blank measures below.
  2. Clap and count the rhythm you created.

Pulse Play

In each of these rhythms:

  1. Tap and count.
  2. Re-write the rhythm in the new meter suggested.
  3. Tap and count the rhythm you wrote. It should sound the same as the first rhythm.

Ear Detective

Your teacher will play the melodies below. Some measures are blank.
In the blank measures write the missing notes you hear.

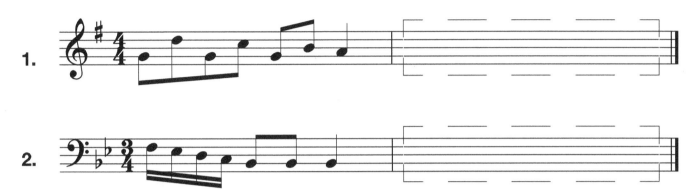

Your teacher will tap one rhythm from each of these pairs.
Circle the pattern you hear.

Your teacher will play one of these scales or modes.
Circle the scale or mode you hear.

1. major	2. major	3. major
natural minor	natural minor	natural minor
harmonic minor	harmonic minor	harmonic minor
pentatonic scale	pentatonic scale	pentatonic scale
blues scale	blues scale	blues scale
Mixolydian mode	Mixolydian mode	Mixolydian mode
Dorian mode	Dorian mode	Dorian mode

Sight-Playing

Before playing each piece, observe the key and time signatures.
Then set a strong rhythmic pulse.

The Old City uses the E _____ mode.

The Old City

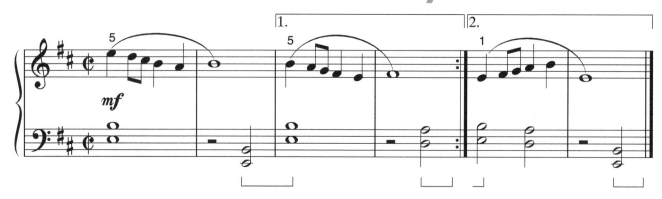

Sorrow is in the key of _____ major / minor (circle one).

Sorrow

Bell Choir is in the key of _____ major / minor (circle one).

Bell Choir

Cross-mode Puzzle

Write the letters for each mode in order.
Be sure to include sharps or flats.

ACROSS (MIXOLYDIAN)

1. D

4. F

6. G

8. C

9. A

DOWN (DORIAN)

2. E

3. C

5. A

6. G

7. D

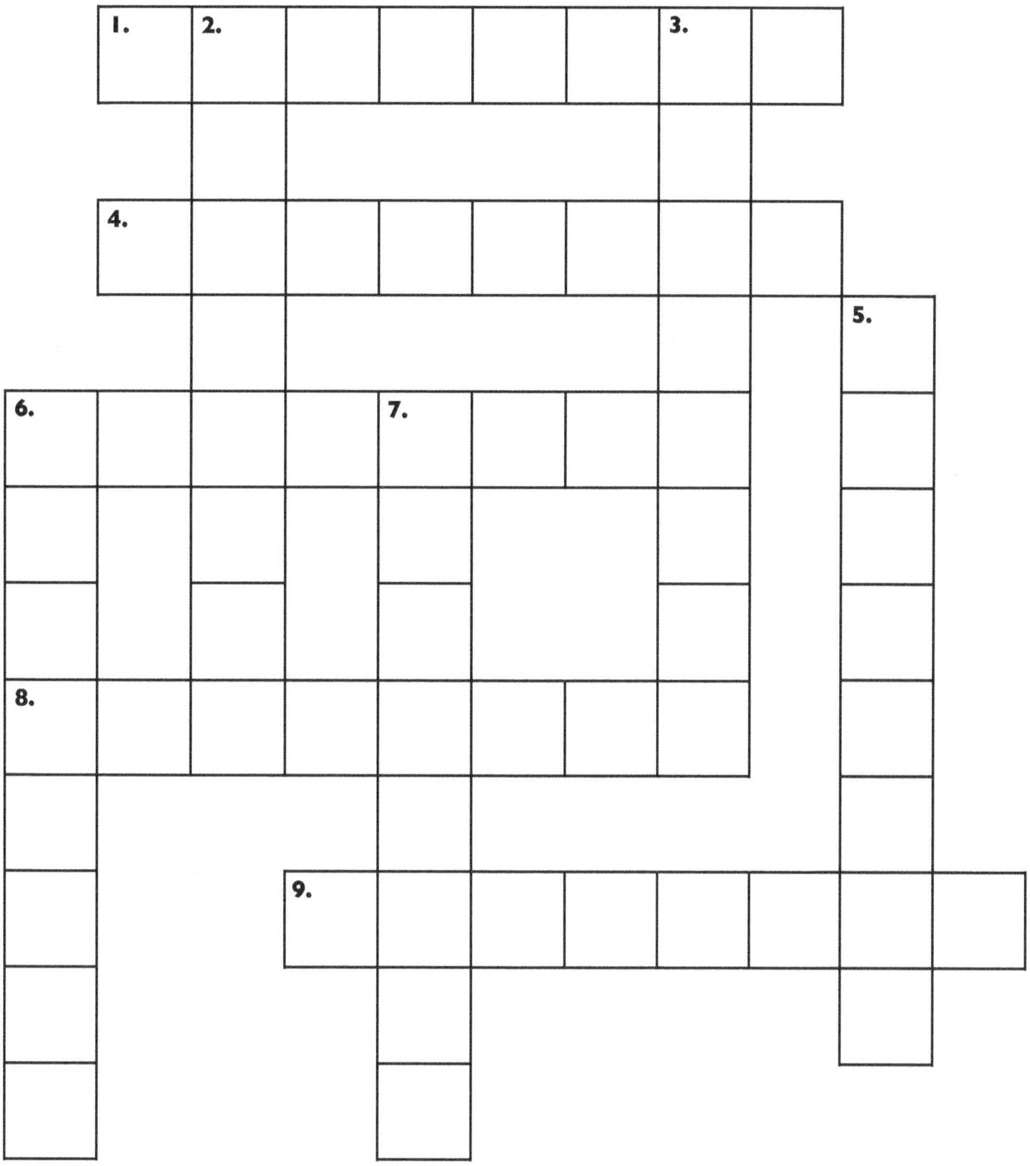

Glossary

two 16th notes	♬	Fill the time of one 8th note
dotted 8th note	♪.	Fills the time of an 8th note tied to a 16th note
dotted 8th and 16th rhythm	♪. ♪	Lasts as long as one quarter note
common time	**C**	Another way to show $\frac{4}{4}$
cut time	**¢**	Another way to show $\frac{2}{2}$
meters with half note pulse	$\frac{2}{2}$ $\frac{3}{2}$ $\frac{4}{2}$	The top number shows the number of pulses in each measure. The bottom number shows that the half note is the pulse.
syncopation		A shift in rhythmic emphasis from a strong part of the pulse to a part that is normally weaker
blues scale		Scale frequently used in jazz music, built with the pattern m3-W-H-H-m3-W. The minor 3rds often change to major.
dominant triad	**V**	Triad built on the fifth degree of any major or minor scale
dominant seventh	**V7**	Often used instead of a dominant triad in accompaniments
Dorian mode		Scale from ancient music, like a natural minor scale except degree 6 is a half step higher
harmonic minor scale		Natural minor scale with degree 7 raised one half step higher
inversions		The rearrangement of the notes of a triad or interval
root position		When the root of the triad is the bottom note of the chord
1st inversion		When the root of the triad is the top note of the chord
2nd inversion		When the root of the triad is the middle note of the chord

key signature		The sharps or flats appearing at the beginning of each staff to indicate the major or minor key of a composition
		D major key signature B minor key signature
		B-flat major key signature G minor key signature
		A major key signature F-sharp minor key signature
		E-flat major key signature C minor key signature
letter symbols	**A, Dm, C/G,** etc.	A way to show which triad or inversion to play when accompanying a melody
major scale		Eight tones arranged in alphabetical order; made of whole steps except for half steps between degrees 3-4 and 7-1
Mixolydian mode		Scale from ancient music, like a major scale except degree 7 is a half step lower
natural minor scale		Scale made of whole steps except for half steps between degrees 2-3 and 5-6
pentatonic scale		Scale using five notes. It is like a major scale without degrees 4 and 7
relative keys		Major and minor keys that share the same key signature. Tonic for the relative minor is the 6th degree of the major scale.
subdominant triad	**IV**	Triad built on the fourth degree of any major or minor scale
tonic triad	**I**	Triad built on the first degree of any major or minor scale